ABOUT THE LEXI RUDNITSKY EDITOR'S CHOICE AWARD

The Lexi Rudnitsky Editor's Choice Award is a collaboration between Persea Books and The Lexi Rudnitsky Poetry Project. It sponsors the annual publication of a poetry collection by an American who has published at least once previous full-length book of poems. The Editor's Choice Award is the second collaboration between Persea and the Lexi Rudnitsky Poetry Project, following the Lexi Rudnitsky First Book Prize in Poetry, awarded annually to an American woman who has yet to publish a book. Both awards are conducted via contest. Entry guidelines are available on Persea's website.

Lexi Rudnitsky (1972–2005) grew up outside of Boston, and studied at Brown University and Columbia University. Her own poems exhibit both a playful love of language and a fierce conscience. Her writing appeared in *The Antioch Review, Columbia: A Journal of Literature and Art, The Nation, The New Yorker, The Paris Review, Pequod*, and *The Western Humanities Review*. In 2004, she won the Milton Kessler Memorial Prize for Poetry from *Harpur Palate*.

Lexi died suddenly in 2005, just months after the birth of her first child and the acceptance for publication of her first book of poems, *A Doorless Knocking into Night* (Mid-List Press, 2006). The Lexi Rudnitsky book prizes were created to memorialize her by promoting the type of poet and poetry in which she so spiritedly believed.

Previous winners of the Lexi Rudnitsky Editor's Choice Award:

2012   Mitchell L. H. Douglas   *blak al-febet*
2011   Amy Newman   *Dear Editor*

Vermeer in Hell | *Michael White*

POEMS   Winner of the 2012 Lexi Rudnitsky Editor's Choice Award

A Karen & Michael Braziller Book   PERSEA BOOKS | NEW YORK

Persea Books, Inc.
277 Broadway
New York, NY 10007

Library of Congress Cataloging-in-Publication Data

White, Michael, 1956–
[Poems. Selections]
Vermeer in Hell : poems / Michael White.—First edition.
        pages cm
"Winner of the Lexi Rudnitsky Editor's Choice Award."
"A Karen & Michael Braziller Book."
Includes bibliographical references.
ISBN 978-0-89255-436-2
I. Title.
PS3573.H47445A6 2014
811'.54—dc23
                    2014003943

First edition
Printed in the United States of America
Designed by Rita Lascaro

CONTENTS

I.
Coup _ 3

II.
On Highland Road _ 9

View of Delft _ 10

The Girl With a Pearl Earring _ 12

Anniversary _ 15

Officer with Laughing Girl _ 17

Out Back _ 19

Bioluminescence _ 20

Girl With a Red Hat _ 21

Woman Holding a Balance _ 22

The Molesworth Group _ 25

The Little Street _ 26

Woman in Blue Reading a Letter _ 29

The Milkmaid _ 31

Anne Frank's Tree _ 36

Woman Holding a Pearl Necklace _ 38

III.
Vermeer in Hell _ 41

Notes _ 55

Acknowledgments _ 57

About the Author _ 58

Coup

(Wilmington, NC)

Everyone goes for an evening walk
next to the Cape Fear's roiled & dented current
sidling past, as little rivulets

of melting praline ice cream drip down the sides
of the waffle cone I'm usually holding here.
Last Sunday, Sophia spotted a longnosed gar

with delicate, attenuated bowsprit
ghosting upstream just beside this wharf.
We followed it. How well the river fits

the city: white stone facing the tea-black tide,
the gutted ribs of hulls, sunk bones of piers
half risen once again on the other side.

Not much has changed, I think. Sometimes I imagine
10 November, 1898—
the thud of a rifle butt at 8 a.m.

on the door of the *Daily Record*. Post election
Thursday morning. Colonel Waddell backed
by his white mob. You have to expect someone

would knock down lanterns, someone find a match.
The pop & whoosh of upper story windows,
flurries of sparks, then suddenly the crash . . .

You have to imagine cheers, their soaring hearts.
Therefore the march on Brooklyn—the colored section
whites called "darktown"—where, within an hour

a shout a shot a fusillade let fly
on a group of blacks on the porch of Walker's Store.
Some died where they fell, the others ran away,

but the infantry was called out anyway;
& Captain James, on the 4th Street Bridge to Brooklyn,
told his machine gun squad to "shoot to kill,"

& neighborhood churches, parks, & black-owned houses
everywhere were targets. Panic spread
from block to block like a sheet of wind-fanned flame.

Dan Wright was burned out, forced to run the gauntlet—
forty guns let loose at his back while his
wife, pleading, watched. Josh Halsey, trapped at last,

was forced to run the gauntlet—forty guns
"tore off the top of his head," as someone said,
while his young daughter watched. Imagine a woman

peering out through the drawn blinds of her living
room, as every prayer she had ever known
flits in & out of her mind. Her baby cries,

as just outside, the horse-drawn Gatling crew
takes aim: each burst of rounds like the Holy Ghost,
like the hieroglyphs of stars. So everyone who

could run ran—four thousand women & children
exiled into swamps & graveyards. Dante
sang of "blackened waters"—city of "wretches

boiled in pitch"—& so Brooklyn became.
By 4 p.m., Waddell was declared mayor.
By 5—gunmetal sundown—what it was

was ghost town: rubble of houses burning, crackle
of sniper fire, a pall of black smoke drifting
down the river. Some of the wounded crawled

beneath their own homes, & were found by the stench
days later. Twenty-five workers, picked off near
the railroad yard, were buried there in a ditch.

But most were left in plain sight: manifestos,
love notes to the future. Streetpole lynchings.
Rigored bodies lying in pools of blood.

"When we turned him over, Misto Niggah
had a look o' 'sprise on his face!" one said.
And what it had been now no longer was—

its bricklayers & drayers, its stevedores
& laundresses—no longer was. No one
came back. And yet it is so beautiful here:

the whole dusk taken in, the whole dusk given
back again, as livid strokes of cloud
& drawbridge laved across the bronze-green dark.

One of the last men killed that night was killed
right here, on Water Street. Two white men claimed
an unnamed black had "sassed" them. Therefore they shot him;

therefore they "tossed his body off the dock,"
where fathers & daughters ramble, & lovers talk,
& everyone goes for an evening walk.

__ II. __

On Highland Road

The wilderness at the end of the road
was sumac, cattails & poison oak—
a susurrus of ghosts in my head,

a smoldering dusk of livid blood
above the faded redwood decks
of the brick tract homes on Highland Road.

I knelt beside the creek & stared
at a single, pristine raccoon track,
till something snapped in the back of my head,

as a transformer on a pole exploded
there in the sky, with a fiery crack—
a ball of flames at the end of the road.

Then I ran home to tell my dad
(adrift in a haze of cigar smoke)
before I could think it was all in my head,

& led him by the hand outside,
& pointed westward at the smoke—
still hanging there, at the end of the road—
but it was gone, it was all in my head.

View of Delft

Storm clouds gather at the top of the canvas,
but the eye is drawn beyond, into the distance,

where an immaculate flock of cumulus looms
above the unseen sea. In front of me,

the River Schie slides left to right across
the bottom third of the view—the smoky glass

of harbor, steeples splayed straight down into
the blue of the mirrored sky. Here on this side,

in the left foreground, two women in pleated black—
white bonnets & collars—stand next to the ferry,

one of them cradling a basket. In between
the shadowy river & the luminous clouds

lies Delft—its water gates & barbicans,
a couple of herring boats moored for repairs,

forever, on the right. If there is only
one scene given, graven on a sheet

of water, one hour that cannot be taken
back, I'm thinking, this is it. The clock

on the Schiedam gate reads 7:10—the sky
blurred with a rainy sheen, unraveling like

a misremembered dream. No matter how
decisively the pointillés describe

seams in the stone, the scene, no matter how
invitingly sun warms the unseen center,

what I'm left with, looking back upon
this hour, this loveliness, remains a distance

I can't cross, a city I can't enter.

The Girl With a Pearl Earring

What he sees, what anyone sees
in her huge, olive irises—

the pupil of the nearer one
dilating as it focuses

within arms' reach—is everything dreamt
for once, this once, the apparitional

instant fixed, projected through
the aperture. But it's her mouth

that gives her up, the tip of her tongue,
the glint of her teeth, the glistening of

her lip's frank blush. The greenish glaze
she once bloomed out of has, by now,

been ground down to this state of badly
abraded blackness—heaven or hell,

oblivion. He's chosen an
outlandish, ornamental, vaguely

oriental turban, resembling
nothing anyone ever wore:

a limpid, lapis lazuli headband
tightly wrapped about her brow,

with a pale-gold pendant, like a silken
ponytail trailing behind,

though it seems to be flung just slightly back,
as if with the glance, the turn which is toward

or suddenly away from him . . .
And the pearl itself—invisible, tear-shaped

counterfeit of varnished glass—
hangs pendulous & hardly there

from the softly-shadowed tip of her ear,
barely revealed beneath the scarf.

All there is to it, really, is
a fluid, comma-like, deliberate

stroke of white that registers
the rake of light on its left-hand curve,

while a duller, horizontal mark
delineates the underside,

reflecting the single swathe of her collar
just beneath. There's nothing else:

the thing itself too immaterial,
too ethereal to be

set down in our own space or time.
And so, love's face—this first glance, last glance,

contextless, accusatory—
comprehends beyond forgiveness,

looks back, but it's too late. Touch
& retouch of the pearl. The instant

passes, in notation of
the umber cloak, the ochre pendant,

turban glazed a deep, transparent
ultramarine upon an opaque

ultramarine. If he *does* stop,
he stops for the thunderous tonnage of

the carillon in the Nieuwe Kerk tower,
whose pealing tremors resonate

through brick & pane as he waits. Now
he dips & loads his badger brush

with cream & earth & cinnabar,
then gradually smoothes her still-wet cheek,

her lips shot with red madder. When
the bristles of his attention fray,

when they get stuck in the scrub of paint,
he leaves them there with his signature.

Maybe then there's a last touch. Maybe
then there's a last touch after that.

Anniversary

Came to, witless, racked in hospital—
some sort of hospital, where inmates shuffled
to & fro in gowns & slippers. Others

huddled motionless, like frostbite victims
waiting for the blood to flow back into
each numb limb again. That first day, what

I focused on, as wave on wave of tremors
shuddered up the shins of chairs, was how
a cigarette could save me. Still, how hard

it was to grasp the simplest things: for instance,
it was summer. Look, it's summer, I thought,
staring out the dayroom window: there

where sheets of lightning traced the contours of
the river hills, out where the Plains begins.

*

Suddenly, on the third day, voices came through.
"Lord, make me a channel of Thy peace,"
said a guy with IV, swatting invisible flies.

"That where there is hatred, I may bring love," said a tattooed
girl-prince, hiding her bruise-brown tracks. I tried
to follow the turns of verse, but the words seemed to

keep sliding away the more I stared at them.
I could say this was the moment, this was it,
but all that really sank in was the gravelly

note in that man's throat, the same in hers,
the same in mine, the sense that all we were
was pain, each couplet circling back again,

like the fiery sparks of dust motes swirling through
that slant of sunlight, twenty-five years ago.

Officer and Laughing Girl

The offhand slash of his hat & shoulder sash;
the present moment, here & now come calling.
Massive knuckles crumpled against one hip,
his back a wall of shadow-scarlet, scarlet
longcoat flaring beneath the table. Merest
glint of an eye. Bolt upright, withheld.
                                        She,
on the other hand, leans forward, offering
her wren-like self, her awkwardly rouged lips
& cheeks, &—this is my favorite part—her lazy
right eye drifting a little out, beyond . . .

I back off. There's an antique chair before me—
sentinel below the painting—tasseled
gold rope draped across it. I'm thinking of
the great age of the everyday, the ribald
tavern scenes, the merry companies . . .

For here is something truly unexpected:
purity, arrayed in the richly embroidered,
black & yellow gown—its sleeves festooned
with gold-braid pointillés—triangulated
in her smile, her open left palm lying
perfectly relaxed & beckoning
on the table. Sunlight strikes the open casement,
blazoning each beveled pane, then floods
the illustrated, gold & robin's-egg-
blue map of Holland, hanging on the room's
rear wall. A startling clarity that sees
straight through him, through his unreflective silence,
sees through me as well. I feel lightheaded,
here in the Frick, as if I'd risen from
the dead, or managed to peer, by some strange spell,
into a dream where everything & nothing

happens. All I know, all anyone knows,
is what we see: love's face in a luminous trance
of space, love's face as it is, brimful of sun,
& we only know what we see because we've seen it.

Out Back

I'm bent down, prying the bird bath
basin up on edge,
in order to roll it back

uphill to its pedestal.
Meanwhile, my homemade wind-chimes
clank. Sidelong, I notice,

underneath the azaleas,
barbwire strands of greenbriers
twining the lower limbs.

And, farther back, this winter's
squirrels have scattered hoards
of blackened pecans on

the trampoline—I don't
know why. O for a whiff
of rotten selvage, all

the news from your yard, you think?
—Elizabeth, I'm onto
you, your muzzle breaking

the crust of loam, beloved
ears my hand remembers—
stay down, stay down, hush

my darling, past is past.

Bioluminescence

Seconds passed. I watched one wave approach,
rolling through waters lit with jellyfish,
rolling obliquely landward till it crashed,
its ghostly aura scrawled across the beach.
And though I'd never seen a night that burned
with such intensity, it was your grace
that filled the room, your sleepy, owl-bright gaze
that followed as I closed the blinds. I turned,
& without thinking, pressed my face between
your breasts, where I could hear each lung draw air,
where I could hear the doors of your heart open
& shut methodically beneath my ear.
And nothing like this happened again. And yet
it happened then. It happened. I was there.

Girl With a Red Hat

She's painted on oak panel, directly over
a portrait by someone else, her saturate scarlet

hat absorbing light, her azure robe
dispersing it. A moment's thought, it's tempting

to think—as if he couldn't help himself.
Her eyes, black-irised & unadorned beneath

the incandescent hat, give nothing back.
It's less about him seeing her, I think,

& more the simple fact of being seen—
maybe just once, but truly seen—her glance

projected on the wall of his booth (except
turned upside down & reversed). The luminous, wreathing,

white smoke of her scarf, the blue cape's out-
of-focus chaos of reflection . . . Here,

this once, she's lit from our right, the image caught
as it blooms out of the abstract, freehand

décor. She turns, she looks, & suddenly,
her nostrils flare. Meanwhile, the rest of her face

dissolves, as in a convex lens, & only
her mouth—its glistening, radical succulence,

its glint of teeth, poised tip of the tongue—yes, only
her mouth seems real to us, but real enough

to speak to us through the shadowy seas of love.

Woman Holding a Balance

If the painting-within-the-painting, hanging on the wall
        behind the standing woman,

with its sinners wailing at Christ's feet on Judgment Day—
        if *that* might be one way

of looking at it, then the woman herself, who half
        obscures the painting, is

another. All we know of her is what we see:
        how—weightless, effortless

as flame—she stands to face the lightfall over the umber,
        oilcloth-covered table.

How each of the nails on her right hand, at the center of
        the composition, burns

like phosphor. How—what word would one use? *Beneficent?*—
        her aspect is: the source

of light beneath her skin, such sweetly sculptural eyelids
        & cheekbones, blessing of

her waistline's fullness. Objects here are neither more
        nor less than what they seem

to be: the table, for instance, offering itself,
        the ornate carvings of

its vase-shaped legs, to the benediction of her touch,
        her left-hand fingertips

alight on its very edge. Or the strand of pearls, with its yellow
satin ribbon, furled

all but unnoticed on the oilcloth there, where three
gold coins, & a silver one,

have casually been placed. The woman focuses
on the equilibrium of

the scales, which contain nothing except sun-glint. Now
the shadow-hand—the almost

subliminal shadow caressing the left side of her linen
bonnet—lends support

to her head, as she leans gently back against the hand.
Behind her, on the wall,

the Bosch-like spirits writhe in faceless terror. Christ,
in his golden nimbus, floats

above their heads. But it barely registers—the Judgment
scene, the reckoning—

as relevant, in light of *her,* her certitude
suspended in the air

from thumb & index finger. It won't come again,
this equipoise between

the figure & the room. Vermeer is thirty-two—
the death-carts creaking through

the black smoke of North Europe. Twenty-four thousand dead
in Amsterdam this year.

In June, the war with England will resume. So it
won't come again, I'm thinking,

not with such full-bodied ease. But for the moment,
here she stands. Is realized.

The Molesworth Group

closed in the familiar way: *who you*
see here, what you hear here, when you leave here,
let it stay here. So I'll just say her blue

gaze cut straight through me, in my folding chair;
I'll say I clung to every syllable
she uttered. Later, four of us crossed the heart

of Dublin. All the pubs, unmoored by dusk,
were casting off, the voice in my ear the one
that quietly intoned the regimen

of Haldol, Clozaril, & Thorazine
that kept him tethered in the full moon, musk
of tulips rising from their beds somewhere

unseen in Merrion Square till, at the turn
to my hotel, we stopped, & left it there.

The Little Street

One must step carefully here, such love
      laid down like the palpable weight of brick:

dead lull of an afternoon blocked out
      in springtime, 1657,

seen from across a canal & a street.
      And love has lent the scene a rhythmic,

linear plane of bricks & leaded
      windowpanes, with long, articulate

riverbeds of cracks that spread
      across the fascia—each one chinked,

painstakingly, with lead-white paint
      coarse as the actual mortar. Love

has left these keyhole views for us
      as well: the central door wide open

on a narrow passageway
      with a maidservant at the end of it

bent over a washbasin—sly trickle
      of silvery water draining back

toward the eye in a trough at the side.
      In another door, to the right, a woman

sits, embroidery in her lap,
      her dusty boy & bonneted girl

crouched on the walk beneath a bench
     —both focused raptly there, it's clear,

but on what I can't tell. The sky,
     to the left, is framed with V's of roofs

& gables, smudged-white North Sea clouds
     roughed in as they scud past above.

The eye, the aperture, mulls over
     how the street has worn to this

thin, corrugated sheen in front
     of entrances; how the whitewashed backs

of the benches bear the evidence
     of human hours (one at the left

inscribed *Vmeer* in ligature);
     how the freshly painted streetside shutters—

slate, gray-olive, russet—fade
     to gray on the second floor, while the tiny

attic casement & shutters loom
     almost transparent, color of thought.

It's springtime, 1657.
     None of the men have come home yet.

The maidservant dries her hands in her skirt,
     as the mother gathers her sewing up,

calls to her children to come inside,
& everything else goes on.

Woman in Blue Reading a Letter

that someone has apparently just brought to her.
I step away, then lean

back in. Then step away. Then lean back into the breathless
hush of pearl again,

where everything about her burns a different shade
of blue: her lunar morning

jacket, rumpled folds of the linen tablecloth,
the granular blue air.

She hovers, motionless, a little out of focus,
one page tightly clasped

as she reads, the other laid on the corner of the table,
partially covering

the strand of pearls she was about to try on. On
the whitewashed wall behind her

hangs a vast, mysterious map of consciousness
itself, I think, for there are

no compass points, no cities nor place-names given to guide us,
only the in-between,

the estuarine wastes of dream. I stare & stare at the plaster
wall, where luminous waves

of gold slide left to right approaching her, where umbral
waves of blue slide left

to right away from her, her lips parted, as phrase
by phrase, she parses out

the voice in her mind. For another minute now,
I look at this bell-shaped cloud

of lapis balanced perfectly within itself,
then turn, descend two flights

of steps, & almost immediately lose myself
in the vaporous, half-lit city.

The Milkmaid

How small the dreaming figure from across
the room in the Rijksmuseum. How calm the fact

of her lowered gaze, the open breadth of her brow.
As I move closer, though, each brushstroke of

impasto separates into the red-browns,
grays & lead-whites of her actual skin.

The vigorous, chalky pentimenti of
her sinewy forearms, arced half-consciously

with the weight of the pitcher, as if with the weight of a baby.
Gold-encrusted bread loaves. Ultramarine

of her apron, pure crushed lapis lit in full sun.
Lead-tin yellow of her blouse, with woven,

darker flecks of ochre. All this while,
a blue-white trickle of milk backs up at the lip

of the pitcher, slips across, then ribbons down
& down into the stoneware bowl. But the eye

can only hold so much before it wanders,
over the pockmarked, plaster wall behind her,

picking out the minute, bluish shadow
each nail casts to the right beside itself—

each menial smudge, each mark of love. The window's
watery, iris-blue panes undulate

as I pore over the missing piece, the hole
in one of them, which lets in a freezing draft . . .

It's winter outside, solid ice across
the black canal, but when I lean in close

& peer out through the broken pane, it's April
out there, it's the next day, & it isn't

Amsterdam, but Delft: sun-dappled, bronze-green
water, hyacinths blooming everywhere

in window-boxes & on the stern of a houseboat
disappearing off to the right. I'm walking

down Vermeer's street, the Oude Langendijk,
which is empty, except for a woman pedaling toward me,

wicker basket slung on her handlebars.
And a younger girl, a redhead, sits on a step

a few feet away from me, a cigarette burning
in her right hand, her chin propped in the left—

a student, I'd guess, from Delft University,
in silver lamé flip-flops, olive skirt

half-gathered about her knees, black tights & bra-straps.
Without breaking stride, I click the shutter,

holding the camera waist-high as I pass,
her cigarette an inch from my left thigh,

just as the cyclist whizzes past, an inch
to the other side. A glance toward the blur of tire

tan knee white skirt on my right, then back to the girl,
the ash of her cigarette that doesn't move,

her gaze that does not move as my foot comes down
& I enter her line of sight, still focused sidelong

up the street, & pass. Invisible,
I think. And it wouldn't be right to look back at

her shock of red hair burning against the dark glass
as I pass over humpbacked bridges with white handrails,

through the west gate of old Delft. The milk of her skin,
an hour perhaps of sun still wicking out—

a blanket, wine, small talk—an hour beneath
the willows, I think, crossing the Stationplein

to the stairs to the platform back to Amsterdam.

*

But now, months later, staring at the shot
on my screen, I'm suddenly not so sure. Her hair

is dyed, of course—a saturate cinnamon
or plum—but her fringes, arching primly across

her temple, are freshly trimmed; her nails are lacquered
& almond-shaped. When she stands & smoothes her skirt,

she'll look professional & chic. Reflected
in the glass above are these faint words

in English: "hair" & "fashion" & "magazines."
It's *hers*, I realize—*her* shop, *her* sky,

her street—as much as it was ever *his*,
Vermeer's. The gilt hands on the Niewe Kerk tower

have stopped today at 4:36, as she waits
on her next appointment. Nothing's going on—

the floor's swept, everything tidied up inside.
I think of the footwarmer on the floor next to

the maid: a simple, clay bowl full of coals
in a wooden box, with holes carved in the top,

where she can rest a foot if she wants. A stick,
to stir the coals, lies nearby on the tiles—

a faint suggestion, nothing more. This maid
fresh from the country. And maybe the stylist is marking

time as well, has better things in mind.
What could be better, I think (middle-aged,

invisible) than what she has: the heft
of stoneware in both hands, the sibilance

of caffa slipping through her fingers? Look
at the weft of what is seen, the crusts we break

& tear with our teeth, & above this—between
us & the scene itself—the specular sheen

of everything she's touched. What could be better,
on the other hand, than what *she* has: this late hour,

shadows welling out of the canal,
the River Schie & the sea? Where is the love

that can match our dream of it? I lower my camera
to my hip—the bike clattering past an inch

to my right, the cigarette an inch to my left.
Here's the song I sing to myself: please let me

pass unnoticed, Lord—if You exist,
if You can hear—let me be no one, nothing,

Lord, as I slip through & disappear.

Anne Frank's Tree

*"Diseased Anne Frank tree to be cut down
next week . . . A graft will be put in its place."*
—Reuters, Nov 13, 2007

A fifteen-year-old girl
on tip-toe in the attic
saw the huge horse-chestnut,

Westerkerk tower, & the random
North Sea gull. "Our tree
is in full blossom . . . even

more beautiful than last year,"
she wrote, on the thirteenth of May,
1944.

A nightingale once built
her nest beside the house
of a poet. He was ill.

He sat beneath a plum
one day, & when he returned,
his hands were filled with the scraps

of stanzas. Here is the plum.
I know I shouldn't, but
I pluck one leaf. I crush it,

place it beneath my tongue,
releasing its bitter mint.
Praise to the angel's wordless

gaze—her angled cut,
her balm of moss—who coaxes
the root, who stakes the shoot

of the chestnut & the plum.

Woman Holding a Pearl Necklace

Here is a girl presented as a fact:
a few stray ringlets at the back of her neck,
the necklace glinting at her throat, drawn taut
on its yellow ribbons. Here is a girl unconscious,
unaware—each fingertip relaxed,
suspended in mid-air—her shadowy gaze
turned toward the light, toward the black-framed mirror hanging
beside the window. Now, because I'm late,
because the museum is closing in fifteen minutes,
I'm trying to burn her figure into my mind:
the gold-foil sheen of her satin gown, the feel
of its ermine trim. I stare & stare at the still-life
of forgotten things—the powder brush
& ivory comb—at the way the daylight lights
each intricately leaded pane, ignites
the plaster inch by inch, till it glows like snow
in the lee of a house, like a high, white North Sea sky
the sun never quite breaks through . . .

                           A guard approaches;
taps his wrist. I nod & lower my head
& walk straight past the Flemish & Italian
suites, outside into the Tiergarten:
dark ponds of geese, the bullet-riddled bust
of Haydn. Four bronze horses paw the air.
I'm suddenly in the wrong clothes: rain like gravel
pelts my face. I can't hold onto her.

__ III. __

Vermeer in Hell

1.

A Girl Reading a Letter by an Open Window

The first of his female figures, rapt at the center of
 her world—maybe the first

& only real discovery he'll ever make.
 She's holding the vellum out

to catch the fall of white-gold light, its edges curled
 & sun-infused, as if

by stages burned away. She's two-thirds down the page,
 & perfectly absorbed,

although she will soon glance up, I think, & stare out through
 the open casement, into

the street & sky. I can't make out the color of
 her eyes, but the fine, tight braids

of her chignon, straw-blonde curls cascading from her temple,
 & her lemon satin bodice

trimmed with black, all ravish me. Vermeer shields her
 discreetly, with a massive

still-life, featuring a blue & white Wan-Li bowl
 overflowing with fruit,

one ripe peach already halved. There's an Ushak carpet
 rucked up on the left,

& a shimmering, green trompe-l'oeil curtain drawn partway
across the scene on the right.

Meanwhile, a grade-school class files in, sits down on the floor,
the teacher begins. I wander

off for an hour, as tour group after tour group enters:
Czech, then Japanese . . .

Later, I've settled back. A high, white North light slants
down through the window in

the room I'm standing in, as a high white North light slants
down through the window in

the room *she's* standing in—the same light lighting her letter
lights this page in my journal.

Purchased, as a Rembrandt, in 1742,
by Augustus III,

for his Dresden pleasure-palace. When I look up again,
the afternoon has passed.

She hasn't moved, she hasn't breathed, as I back off.
She's two-thirds down the page.

2.

Passing through the Zwinger gardens—balustrades & plumes
of fountains—straight out through the Glockenspiel Pavilion

where I pause to read an inscription on a marble tablet:

13 Feburar 1945
Vernichteten Anglo-Amerikanische Bomberverband die Innenstadt Dresdens

but I don't read the rest, I turn left, follow the Sophienstrasse
into the Theatreplatz, its surface paved

with round, black stones—a sheen of midsummer showers
where fat, black pigeons stroll before my feet

where the Opera, Schloss, & Hofkirche hunch like beetles around the
    square,
their ornate, veined elytra drawn protectively around them

where the August-Brucke hopscotches the Elbe, its seven arches
still smoke-black in the middle

where yesterday—Friday—afternoon, 700 skinheads in black T-shirts
crossed en masse, just as I arrived from Berlin

where on my right a vast staircase ascends the air
like a waterfall of stone

where the sky burns blue above the town, where the dusk slides leaden—
black swans, manes of horses

where I remember seeing these stairs in a black-&-white photo
of a wholesome blonde in braids in 1935

where next to her—mid-flight, at the rail—a huge sign said:
Juden Zutritt Verboten

where I find myself on the Bruhl Terrace—the river shivering
at my left, the Altstadt at my right

baroque cupolas, smoke-black angels hovering silently above
the Elbflorenz—this Florence on the Elbe

3.

I feel a shadow behind me. A paddle steamer bearing the name
"Augustus the Strong" is moored below, in the swerve of river.
Nothing over the hills beyond.

Then I realize: this was the approach that night, straight up the valley,
over everything I see.

*

As the first wave arrived, at the end of its five-hour journey, the
winter cloud cover opened, as if on cue, over the marvelous city.

At 10:03, the eight Pathfinder Mosquitoes dropped a thousand
sparkling "Christmas Trees"—the white magnesium parachute flares
that children marveled at, from windows & half-open cellar doors.
Then, one by one, the canisters of red flares lit up the soccer field—
the aim-point at the west edge of the Altstadt.

At 10:06, Dresden awash with hovering, incandescent light, the public
speakers first announced: "Achtung, Achtung, Achtung."

*

"Come in & bomb glow of red TI as planned," said the master
bomber, hovering low over the city. "Bomb the glow of red TI's as
planned," to the waiting pilots of Plate Rack Force.

And so, from 10:14 to 10:16, each squadron of heavily laden
Lancasters banked in wingtip to wingtip over the aim point, fanning
out precisely two degrees apart: the ache of tension, bomb-bays open,
everyone crouching holding their breath.

Starboard, steady, steady, steady, said the aimer through the intercom—& *steady now,* the whole crew waiting for the *thrum-thrum-thrum* of the release—

When the calculated mix of air mines, high-explosive bombs, & stick incendiaries tumbled out into the night, plane after plane careened straight up into the sky, & everyone held on, held still, filling their lungs at last—

When 244 bombers—one every 7.5 seconds—let go 881 tons of bombs into the heart of beauty—

"That's good bombing, Plate Rack Force," said the master bomber, as the Lancasters headed home.

*

I'm at the end of the promenade, in the shade of a terraced garden, with steep drop-offs on three sides. I'm looking for a name, a stone, which I don't expect to find. There's no one here. It's pleasant, nearly twilight, laughter wafting up from the bars & cafés in the narrow, curving Münzgasse on the one hand, broken haloes halfway across the river on the other. Breezes toss the lindens at my shoulders.

Here is the marker in my mind:

13 February 1945
Victor Klemperer
Author, Professor, Philologist
One of the last Jews left in Dresden
Survived the Firestorm Here

*

When the second wave of 550 fully laden Lancasters approached at 1 a.m., the airmen could see the glow from a hundred miles away.

One of them, Doug Hicks, wrote: "Almost daylight conditions prevail. The sky is lit up from the horrendous inferno on the ground that is now the target. In this lighted environment I now see bomber aircraft everywhere . . . I have difficulty in comprehending this vast armada of aircraft converging on the target."

Another, Miles Tripp, wrote: "The streets of the city were a fantastic latticework of fire. It was as though one was looking down at the fiery outlines of a crossword puzzle; blazing streets stretched from east to west, from north to south, in a gigantic saturation of flame. I was completely awed by the spectacle."

When the second wave arrived, none of their marker flares could be made out through the blaze & smoke, so in the end, the master bomber ordered the pilots to "bomb the center of the fire."

When the second wave arrived, there was no warning at all.

And everything else, dear Reader, you know.

How everyone took to their cellars, mothers lying atop their children, wrapped in blankets, pressed to the floor, where it seemed some traces of air might be.

How those who stayed in suffocated, waiting for firefighters who were already dead themselves.

How those who went out, went out into the gale-force wind, the actual pillar of flame.

How no one could help the women in maternity wards, the elderly in wheelchairs.

How no one could help the hordes in the Hauptbahnoff, the zoo, & the park, where a steady rain of bombs wailed down through the shattered & exploding trees.

And no one could help the Circus Sarrasani tigers, burning piteously in their cages.

And no one could help the royal Lipizzaners—led through the city by hand that night, in flight from the Eastern front—80 stallions cut to pieces with their grooms.

And yet:

*

Out of thirteen miles of ash & liquefied asphalt,
out of Dis itself, while the Furies howled above,
a 65-year-old man climbed forth,
laboring with bad back, bad heart,
& bleeding profusely from one eye.
A Protestant, & a star-wearing Jew—
his ticket to Auschwitz already punched—
Victor Klemperer climbed this hill, & lived.

4.

When the second wave arrived at 1 a.m.,
Eva roused him & they raced downstairs—
she "two steps ahead" of him—

but just as they reached the courtyard door,
a near hit shattered glass & stone—& when
he stood up, she was gone. He searched the corners

of the Jew's cellar, where women & children
clung to one another, as "bangs, as light
as day, explosions" blew the windows in

& "something hot" had gashed his face. He felt
for his right eye—"it was still there." Then someone,
he never saw who, helped him to his feet

& pushed him out into the throat of the maelstrom.
Showers of blazing firebrands filled the searing
air, the updraft feeding the firestorm

fierce enough to uproot oaks, to wring
each molecule of breath from a blistered lung,
to knock the living off their feet, & fling

them headlong into the cauldron. In the Altstadt,
panic took hold: hundreds fled through fire
to the ten-foot-deep lagoon in the Altmarkt,

where even the strongest clawed in vain when the water
came to a boil. Still others raced
to the killing fields beside the Elbe. But Victor

scrambled up the burning slopes of this terrace
garden. Here it was cooler; here he could breathe.
The view "within a wider radius"

was "nothing but flames." All night, he rode this spit
of rock, & danced to the left, or else to the right,
as the bones of the Elbflorenz turned white-hot

& collapsed in torrents of sparks. All night,
he stood with his satchel full of manuscripts,
his mind a torment: "Why had I not thought

more about her?" All night, as I imagine it,
he soared above the fiery wind—as if
on the back of Geryon, who set

him safely down at last, in the city of
the dead. Ash Wednesday: rubble burning;
river pitch-black; nothing moving. Out of

drizzling rain & shadow—light returning
over the shoulders of the Saxon hills—
he left the shelter of the lindens, trembling

with fatigue, & walked out past the shell
of the Belvedere, onto the terrace. There,
in a group of refugees along the wall,

someone called his name, & it was *Eva*—
Eva sitting unharmed on her suitcase!
Victor held her tighter than he ever

had, as she told of her miraculous
escape. On the bank beneath, as small as ants,
survivors streamed past, burdened with small bundles

or pushing handcarts. Everything was silent—
even the sky hung low & overcast.
The B-17's were coming. This was the moment

Eva opened her pocketknife, & pressed
the point of it into her husband's breast,
& cut the yellow star free from his chest.

5.

It's Sunday—my last afternoon in Dresden—&
the Picture Gallery

is empty. Charm of the young wife's transport as she reads—
her concentration, swathes

of fabric billowing around her, something about
geometry & love

& the fall of daylight onto her brow, as if I hadn't
seen it all before.

Pale ghost of her face as it floats across six panes of glass
in the partly open casement.

Now I lean in, inches from the sculpted surface . . .
Now I notice the bead

of white lead laid along the leading edge of things—
the emerald curtain, lip

of the Wan-Li bowl, the built-up collar at her throat—
the whole scheme burning like

a constellation, separate from its human story.
Thinking about her face,

I turn & walk out through the Zwinger's reconstructed
splendor: glossy parquet,

marble stairway. Dusk, the city's afterlife—
a busker flutes an expert

"Badinerie" beneath the sonorous archways of
the Semperbau. I drop

a coin, then turn to the right this time, the Frauenkirche
reappearing on

my left after a block, its magisterial "stone bell"
reassembled in

its place in the skyline, over GDR slab buildings,
after sixty years.

I'm crossing the Altmarkt, where hundreds of Dresdeners
were "stacked like bricks" each day,

according to the SS officer in charge,
then trampled down, & soaked

with gas, the great pyres smoldering on through spring. Pale ghost
of her face floating in

six panes of glass, her spell unbroken still—because
of her downcast gaze, I think,

or the way each word unfolds in her mind, or because she is only
two-thirds down the page.

"Coup" describes the bloody racist coup that took place in Wilmington, North Carolina, during the election week of 1898. I wrote it in Wilmington, my home, during the election week of 2008. I'm especially indebted to the North Carolina Office of Archives & History for background, and for the eyewitness quotations included here. For more information see http://www.history.ncdcr.gov/1898-wrrc.

The grouping of the Vermeer poems is based partly on location. "View of Delft" and "Girl With a Pearl Earring" are in the Mauritshuis, The Hague. "Officer with Laughing Girl" is in the Frick Museum, New York. "Girl With a Red Hat" and "Woman Holding a Balance" are in the U.S. National Gallery, Washington. "The Little Street," "Woman in Blue Reading a Letter," and "The Milkmaid" are in the Rijksmuseum, Amsterdam. "Woman Holding a Pearl Necklace" is in the Gemäldegalerie, Berlin.

Section 3 of "Vermeer in Hell" is especially indebted to Frederick Taylor's definitive *Dresden: Tuesday, Feb. 13, 1945* for background, and for the eyewitness quotations included here.

Section 4 of "Vermeer in Hell" is especially indebted to the second volume of Victor Klemperer's diaries, published as *I Will Bear Witness (1942–1945)*, for background, and for the Klemperer quotations included here.

ACKNOWLEDGMENTS

"*The Milkmaid*" originally appeared in *The Asheville Poetry Review* as winner of the 2011 William Matthews Poetry Prize.

"*View of Delft*" originally appeared in *The Florida Review* as winner of the 2010 *Florida Review* Editor's Prize.

"Anniversary" and "*Woman Holding a Pearl Necklace*" originally appeared in *Great River Review*.

"Anne Frank's Tree" originally appeared in *Holocaust: A Memorial*, a chapbook from the Publishing Laboratory of The University of North Carolina at Wilmington.

"*Woman Holding a Balance*" originally appeared in *Image: Art, Faith, Mystery.*

"*The Girl With a Pearl Earring*" originally appeared in *The Journal.*

"*Girl With a Red Hat*" and "Out Back" originally appeared in *The Kenyon Review.*

"On Highland Road" originally appeared in *Memorious.*

"Coup" originally appeared in *North Carolina Literary Review.*

"Bioluminescence" originally appeared in *Salt.*

"The Little Street" originally appeared in *Tar River Poetry.*

"*Officer and Laughing Girl*" originally appeared in *Western Humanities Review.*

ABOUT THE AUTHOR

Michael White was educated at the University of Missouri and the University of Utah, where he received his PhD in English. His books include the poetry collections *Palma Cathedral,* which won the Colorado Prize, *Re-entry,* which won the Vassar Miller Prize, and *The Island;* and a memoir, *Travels in Vermeer.* His work has been published in magazines and anthologies including *The Paris Review, The New Republic, The Kenyon Review, Image,* and *The Best American Poetry.* He has received many other awards for his work, including a NEA Fellowship as well as several fellowships from the North Carolina Arts Council. He teaches in the MFA program at the University of North Carolina at Wilmington.